SPOTLIGHT ON
IMMIGRATION AND MIGRATION

THE DISASTER OF THE IRISH POTATO FAMINE

IRISH IMMIGRANTS ARRIVE IN AMERICA (1845–1850)

Sean O'Donoghue

PowerKiDS press.

NEW YORK

Published in 2016 by The Rosen Publishing Group, Inc.
29 East 21st Street, New York, NY 10010

Editor: Caitie McAneney
Book Design: Sarah Liddell

Photo Credits: Cover Universal History Archive/Contributor/Universal Images Group/Getty Images; pp. 5, 17 Northwind Picture Archive; pp. 6, 9 Universal Images Group/Contributor/Universal Images Group/Getty Images; p. 7 Atom Studios/Shutterstock.com; p. 8 Civvi~commonswiki/Wikimedia Commons; pp. 10, 13, 16 Everett Historical/Shutterstock.com; p. 11 Chris 73/Wikimedia Commons; p. 14 Rjensen/Wikimedia Commons; p. 15 FPG/Staff/Archive Photos/Getty Images; p. 18 Cropbot/Wikimedia Commons; p. 19 Magnus Manske/Wikimedia Commons; p. 20 Davepape/Wikimedia Commons; p. 21 (main) SCIENCE SOURCE/Science Source/Getty Images; p. 21 (inset) NASA/Science Source/Getty Images; p. 22 Le Do/Shutterstock.com.

Cataloging-in-Publication Data

O'Donoghue, Sean.
The disaster of the Irish potato famine / by Sean O'Donoghue.
p. cm. — (Spotlight on immigration and migration)
Includes index.
ISBN 978-1-5081-4066-5 (pbk.)
ISBN 978-1-5081-4067-2 (6-pack)
ISBN 978-1-5081-4069-6 (library binding)
1. Ireland — History — Famine, 1845-1852 — Juvenile literature. 2. Famines — Ireland — History — 19th century — Juvenile literature. I. Title.
DA950.7 O36 2016
941.5081—d23

CPSIA Compliance Information: Batch #BW16PK: For further information contact Rosen Publishing, New York, New York at 1-800-237-9932.

CONTENTS

COMING TO AMERICA

In the mid-1800s, it was clear the United States was on the edge of great change. Farms were replaced with steel mills, clothing factories, and other industrial buildings as cities began to grow throughout the country. As the United States underwent its **Industrial Revolution**, **immigrants** from all over the world, especially Europe, arrived hoping to find work and a better life.

One of the largest groups of people to immigrate during this time was the Irish. Between 1845 and 1850, Ireland suffered a terrible agricultural **disaster** when its potato crop was wiped out by **disease**. More than 1 million Irish died during the Potato **Famine**. About another 1 million left Ireland to escape **starvation**. Many had their eyes set on America—a land of hope.

The Potato Famine was also called the Great Hunger. This illustration shows an Irish family inside their small hut during this time.

5

RELYING ON POTATOES

In 1801, Ireland became part of the United Kingdom of Great Britain and Ireland. Throughout the 1800s, the British took most of the land in Ireland as their own.

Many landowners lived in Britain and hired **landlords** to manage their land in Ireland. Most of the Irish were poor and made their living as farmworkers. They rented small plots of land from British landlords, and they paid the high rents on this land by working for the landowners. Irish farmworkers had very little time to work on their own crops, so they grew a lot of potatoes, which were cheap and could grow with little work. Potatoes are also full of nutrients and can grow almost anywhere. Without other food choices, this root vegetable became a key part of the poor Irish diet.

The Irish worked hard to keep a roof over their heads and feed their family. Still, many lived in **poverty**.

SUFFERING IN IRELAND

While the poor Irish farmworkers didn't have much, they could survive on potatoes. However, from 1845 to 1850, most of the potato crop was destroyed by a plant disease called blight. It caused the potatoes to rot and die. With no potatoes to eat, many Irish people starved. Prices for other foods went up because of the potato shortage, and the poor couldn't afford to buy food.

At first, the British government provided some food and jobs to those hit hardest by the famine. They began a program that paid Irishmen to build roads and buildings. However, this meant the men had even less time to plant crops. They were also given little money, which made buying food nearly impossible.

potato
with blight

In some places, lack of food led to **violence**. This illustration shows Irish peasants attacking a government potato store in Galway, Ireland.

HOMELESS AND HOPELESS

Soon after British aid began, it ended. Soup kitchens were organized in early 1847, but they were shut down later that year. The potato harvest in fall 1847 was small but free of blight, and the British government felt the soup kitchens were no longer necessary.

The British government passed a law that required soup kitchens to be paid for by Irish tax money. However, most Irish were already struggling to buy food and pay their high rents. They couldn't afford to pay the extra taxes as well. Armed guards **evicted** thousands of Irish farmers and their families from their farms and homes because they couldn't pay their rent. Many Irish ended up homeless, with no hope of gaining food or shelter.

This Irish family has been evicted from their home.

IRISH ARRIVE IN AMERICA

The poor Irish had two choices: stay in Ireland and starve, or move somewhere else. Many looked to the United States, which was believed to be full of opportunities. They braved the difficult voyage from Ireland to the United States in hopes of a better future.

So many people were leaving Ireland that many **cargo** ships were made into passenger ships. Conditions on the ships were terrible. Food and clean water were scarce, and disease was common. The ships became known as **coffin** ships because so many people died on the journey.

The main ports of arrival were the cities of Boston, Philadelphia, New York, and Baltimore. With little or no money to move around, these port cities became home for many new Irish arrivals.

This photograph shows Irish people on a boat in Queensland, Ireland, ready to travel to America.

NO IRISH NEED APPLY

Irish immigrants met challenges the moment they landed in the United States. In port cities, they were often cheated by runners. Runners made money by carrying immigrants' bags to tenement housing in the city, charging high fees for the service.

Tenements were often the only housing new Irish immigrants could afford. They were buildings with many floors and many families living on each level. Conditions were crowded and dirty.

On top of the poor living conditions, the Irish were also not welcomed in the United States. In fact, when advertisements were placed for jobs, they often ended with "No Irish Need Apply." Many Irish had to beg on the streets for enough money just to survive. Though they'd escaped Ireland, the Irish still dealt with crushing poverty and joblessness.

GROCERY CART AND HARNESS FOR SALE —In good order, and one chestnut horse, 8 years old, an excellent saddle horse; can be ridden by a lady. Also, one young man wanted, from 16 to 18 years of age, able to write. No Irish need apply. CLUFF & TUNIS, No. 270 Washington-st., corner of Myrtle-av., Brooklyn.

As if coming to a new country without money wasn't bad enough, the Irish also faced **prejudice**. Many Americans saw Irishmen as heavy drinkers and violent people.

HARD JOBS

Faced with extreme poverty and little to no savings, most Irish in the United States were desperate for work. However, they had few skills other than farming and usually ended up doing the jobs no one else would do.

Most Irishmen found jobs as laborers, construction workers, deliverymen, or ditch diggers. Many Irishmen fought in the American Civil War, which lasted from 1861 to 1865. Women often worked as servants and maids in wealthy American homes.

Even immigrants who found jobs often lived in small, dirty apartments. The poverty and terrible living conditions led to sickness and early death. Many babies born to Irish immigrants living in New York City in the mid-1800s died. The United States, it seemed, wasn't the place they'd hoped it would be.

This young Irish immigrant is still a child, but she has to work long hours making lace to sell.

This 1870s print shows immigrant tenements in Donovan's Lane near the Five Points neighborhood in New York City. It was known as one of the poorest areas with high criminal activity.

BUILDING STRONG COMMUNITIES

New Irish immigrants faced great prejudice in the United States. While they were disliked by others, the Irish clung to each other for support. They didn't give up under the pressure of hatred. Instead, they became stronger.

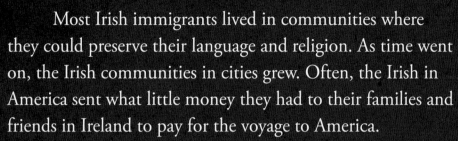

Most Irish immigrants lived in communities where they could preserve their language and religion. As time went on, the Irish communities in cities grew. Often, the Irish in America sent what little money they had to their families and friends in Ireland to pay for the voyage to America.

Over time, the Irish showed they were hardworking. The Irish had finally gained some respect in the United States. Soon, Americans shifted their hatred to the newest arrivals—Jewish and Italian immigrants.

Many Irish Americans held on to their Catholic religion to connect to their home country and culture while building a strong community in the United States. These Irish Civil War soldiers are shown attending a Catholic mass.

FAMOUS IRISH AMERICANS

As time went on, Irish immigrants began to do better in the United States. Their **descendants** found success, and there are many famous Americans who trace their roots to Ireland, or the "Old Sod," as the Irish called it.

Boxing hero John L. Sullivan was born to Irish parents in Boston in 1858. Irish American reporter Elizabeth Jane Cochran, also known as Nellie Bly, made history when she traveled around the world in 72 days in 1889. Bly also went undercover in a mental hospital to expose poor conditions there. John F. Kennedy was perhaps the most famous Irish American of his time. Elected in 1960, he was the first Irish Catholic to become president of the United States. F. Scott Fitzgerald, also of Irish descent, is considered one of the greatest American authors of all time.

John L. Sullivan

Henry Ford, a pioneer in automobile manufacturing, came from an Irish family.

John F. Kennedy

IRISH AMERICANS MAKE THEIR MARK

The Potato Famine forever changed the history of Ireland and the United States. Many Irish had to leave their homes, knowing they'd never see Ireland again.

Today in the United States, there are nearly 33.3 million Irish Americans. Large Irish American communities still exist in big cities, such as New York City, Boston, and Chicago. They're an important part of American society. People across the country celebrate St. Patrick's Day, an Irish holiday, by holding parades and wearing green—the color of Ireland. The four-leaf clover, a **symbol** of Ireland, is seen as good luck. Irish Americans have contributed to American drama, politics, music, and literature. The Irish culture and the struggles of Irish immigrants have made their mark on many areas of American life.

four-leaf clover

GLOSSARY

cargo: Goods carried by a plane, train, or truck.

coffin: A box for burying a dead body.

descendant: A relative of someone from an earlier time.

disaster: An event that causes much suffering or loss.

disease: Illness.

evict: To force someone to leave a place.

famine: A situation in which many people do not have enough to eat.

immigrant: One who comes to a country to settle there.

Industrial Revolution: An era of social and economic change marked by advances in technology and science.

landlord: A person who owns or manages land or a building and rents it to others.

poverty: The state of being poor.

prejudice: An unfair feeling of dislike for a person or group because of race or religious or political beliefs.

starvation: Suffering or death caused by having nothing or not enough to eat.

symbol: Something that stands for something else.

violence: Using force to harm someone.

INDEX

PRIMARY SOURCE LIST

p. 9
Attack on a Potato Store. Creator unknown. Wood engraving. Published in *The Illustrated London News* with article "The Galway Starvation Riots," June 25, 1842.

p. 14
Newspaper ad with "No Irish need apply." Ink on paper. Published in the *New York Times*. March 25, 1854.

p. 19
69th New York State Militia at Church. Created by Mathew B. Brady. Photograph. 1861. Now kept at the Library of Congress Prints and Photographs Division, Washington, D.C.

WEBSITES

Due to the changing nature of Internet links, PowerKids Press has developed an online list of websites related to the subject of this book. This site is updated regularly. Please use this link to access the list: www.powerkidslinks.com/soim/irish